OVERFLOW

How to splash out the Good News

Philip A Clarke

CLIFF COLLEGE
PUBLISHING

This publication has replaced "Evangelism and the local church",
and some of the material appeared in that title.

British Library Cataloguing in Publication Data.
A catalogue record for this book is available
from the British Library.

ISBN 1 898362 23 8

Printed by:

MOORLEY'S Print & Publishing
23 Park Rd., Ilkeston, Derbys DE7 5DA
Tel/Fax: (0115) 932 0643

from data supplied on disk

OVERFLOW

How to splash out the Good News

1. NOTHING TO DECLARE?

A new baby, passing your driving test, your team winning the championship – sharing good news is the most natural thing in the world – you just can't keep it to yourself. The Gospel is Good News, the greatest news ever, yet Christians often feel inhibited in declaring it.

Early in my ministry I was invited to attend the opening of a training centre for evangelists in a remote Cumbrian village with the unfortunate name of Mouthlock! That says it all! Many churches are reasonably effective at 'being there' and doing the deed for the sake of Christ. They are ineffective at naming the Name and giving a reason for the hope that is within them.[1]

Much of the training offered to those preparing for ordination over many generations has been geared to producing teachers and pastors rather than evangelists. Indeed there are those who enter theological training and the early years of ordained ministry as evangelists but lose their zeal for mission through pressure to maintain the system and become increasingly church focused – chaplains to the faithful, keepers of the aquarium more than fishers of people. The church does need pastors and teachers but it also needs the whole five-fold ministry of Ephesians 4, which gives evangelism a high priority.

> Ephesians 4:11-12: "He (Christ) gave some to be apostles, some to be prophets, some to be evangelists and some to be pastors and teachers, to prepare God's people for works of service, so that the body of Christ may be built up." (NIV)

For too long the roles of pastor and evangelist have been kept separate. Today more than ever the need is for pastor-evangelists, rooted in the local church situation, caring for 'the flock', mobilising, equipping and enabling them for mission. Most growing churches have a leadership team which combines pastoral ministry and mission enterprise. Our churches need leaders who themselves model evangelistic ministry and who share a vision with their congregations, allowing individuals to use their gifts, to take risks, to break the mould in order to share the faith.

That may seem like a pipe dream in situations where churches are locked into maintenance mode rather than positively facing the challenge of mission in a secular society, but it is surprising how the vision and prayers of a few can change things.

Many of our churches, even where there is some awareness of mission, look more like yachting clubs than lifeboat stations. There is friendship, organisation, many activities, some generous givers .... but few are rescued.

There are a number of reasons for this:

1. Although we realise that less than 10% of the British population attend church regularly, the church persists with an assimilation model instead of a conversion model. If not actually expressed, the thought is that "if we can keep our Sunday School children we'll survive", instead of a more intentional evangelistic strategy. Church Growth strategies tend to concentrate mainly on the fringe of the church at the expense of the Gospel of the Kingdom for **all** creation[2]. We need a wider vision for what God could do among us and through us among those who have never heard the Christian story.

   Too often the church appears to be saying, "We're here, come and meet us on our terms and you'll be most welcome". The days are long gone when we could rely on a 'come' model. We don't live in Christendom. We need to return to the apostolic model of declaring the Good News to those who have never heard it in a style that connects with twenty-first century society and in the power of the Spirit – "Go into all the world and preach the Gospel."[3] Amidst this zeal to evangelise there will be a concern to nurture, equip and encourage those within the fold. The pastoral and the evangelistic tasks go hand in hand.

2. Resources and training for preachers are probably more advanced now than ever, yet most seem unable to communicate the Gospel with clarity, relevance and vitality. Many people in the pew rarely hear a clear and compelling account of what Christ offers. The message is couched in terms that they do not relate to. This leads to a further problem -

3. Many Christians find it very difficult to share their faith, partly because they may be unsure of what they believe. Discouraging responses in the past have made them feel embarrassed and incompetent. Consequently some have given up the idea of personal witness other than through a Christian lifestyle, and some pluralist theology has made them wonder whether it matters anyway. Others are willing to be 'up front' about faith but have lived within the orbit of the church for so long that they have lost touch with what life is like 'outside'. What they do communicate to non-Christians is untranslatable into the life of most people.

Without resorting to superficial optimism, it is clear that among many people today there is spiritual openness. Despite this interest (which often takes the form of a kind of benign pluralism) there is much naivety regarding the basics of the Christian message and the dangers of pursuing certain mystical or occult activities. We can only address this challenge and opportunity by taking risks and being church in new ways. Traditional institutions with steady leadership often move slowly and resist change with the risks this entails.

In the history of aviation the Wright brothers had many prototypes crash. One sign of a live church is its list of failures: ideas which have been tried but, sooner or later, have been unsuccessful. Many leaders and churches fear failure and therefore never embark on anything very specific or ambitious. If the alternative to taking risks is inactivity which leads to slow but steady decline, have we an alternative? This does not mean that we jump on the latest bandwagon or embrace the current gimmick but it does mean that we will look to seize God-given opportunities when they arise.

The Holy Spirit is the One who frees us to share our faith. The joy and conviction He puts within us cannot be contained. This spontaneity seems sadly lacking in many churches and their leaders and consequently opportunities are missed. So a renewal of our spiritual lives in the power of God's Holy Spirit is foundational to effectiveness in outreach. The Spirit brings deeper faith and larger vision to move mission forward. It is from the overflow of the Spirit that mission springs.

We may decide to close our old church building and move into something like a shop which is more accessible to the community at large. We may plant a new congregation in a home or a public building in an area where there is no place of worship already. We may take the Gospel on to the streets of our town in a celebration march or engage in open air praise in parks or shopping centres. Perhaps we could employ a youth evangelist to work alongside our own members in reaching teenagers or find a house in which a Seed Team could be accommodated for a year of neighbourhood outreach. Perhaps, most significantly, you can train up your local church members in how to share their faith, using one of several excellent resources available through the Methodist Church or Bible Society. Coffee groups in homes to which friends and neighbours can be invited and at which the Gospel is sensitively presented can be most effective. The whole area of mission can be highlighted by the visit of a mission team perhaps from Cliff College. You might give specific training to your own circuit preachers in evangelistic preaching and use them in a specific period of mission. But beware! Any project which does not enable 'ordinary' Christians to share their faith is fatally flawed. It is all too easy to be so heavily committed to a project that personal faith sharing is forgotten.

Encourage every Christian to tell their own story of coming to faith. They may feel their story is unimpressive but most people will relate to something which sounds normal and real; the genuine article is easily spotted. People need to be affirmed in realising that their experience of Jesus is valid and is worth sharing. The testimony of someone who comes to faith very gradually and avoids giving the impression of having 'arrived' spiritually will get through to many people whose pilgrimage is more to do with gradual process than sudden crisis. An Emmaus Road more than a Damascus Road.

All this without asking basic questions about the way our church functions today will seem to some like rearranging the deckchairs on the Titanic. We need to understand the processes at work in our society and actively seek to apply the Gospel to a constantly changing situation. Eddie Gibbs states "The church is still structured to meet the ministry demands of a churched culture, when in reality it should be developing new structures to tackle the missionary challenges of a predominantly unchurched culture"[4]. Lyle Schaller and Kennon Callaghan state: "The day of the professional minister is over, the day of the missionary pastor has come. The day of the churched culture is over, the day of the mission field has come."[5] Here 'professional minister' is interpreted as the minister who is entirely concerned with meeting the internal needs of his or her local church. The 'missionary pastor' is the leader whose pastoral care of the faithful enables them to focus on outreach.

George Barna states: "We currently develop churches based on a model of ministry that was developed several hundred years ago, rejecting the fact that the world for which the model was designed no longer exists. The constant cry of the unchurched, 'The church is irrelevant to the way I live', cannot be addressed until the model itself is renewed to acknowledge that times have changed."[6]

Barna's use of the term 'renewed' or renewal in fact points towards a remedy - a thoroughly scriptural remedy. Mission is only effective through the Holy Spirit and the renewal He brings. In parts of our church this renewal has taken hold but many churches and leaders seem to have been by-passed by a movement widely regarded as the most significant across all denominations this century. The reasons for this must include institutional fatigue and sleeping leadership. An openness to the gifts and ministries of the Holy Spirit amongst the leadership: ministers, local preachers, stewards, will be one way in which the mission of the whole church will be renewed, though the evidence of history is that renewal is hardly ever containable within the old parent structure. Jesus' parable of the new wine requiring new wineskins has alarming and deeply challenging implications for the historic denominations.[7] All evangelism and nurture of new Christians must grapple with this.

Practically speaking, what can a minister do to mobilise the local church for mission? Michael Green[8] offers these pointers: "Have a passion for outreach, teach it, preach it, model it. Encourage prayer, friendship, love and concern for the neighbourhood in the congregation, offer good worship (no one style is right or wrong), build a strong and varied leadership team, appoint God's choice of leaders through prayer and the gifting of the Spirit. Encourage openness to the Spirit. Involve people and use their gifts. Offer training in personal evangelism. Be in touch with non-church people and alive to God."

Churches which are prepared to take seriously the cultural shift from being a predominantly church society to one which is unchurched must recognise their need to turn inside out! In other words, the focus of attention will not be on running programmes in order to gather the congregation together, but on equipping God's people to participate in God's mission as they declare God's message to his world.

The gathering of the church will be to celebrate what God is doing through them in the world, to renew and refocus that mission, and to equip the membership by providing personal support and training appropriate to their gifts.

Most churches need a renewal in the power of the Holy Spirit which is focused not just on certain special events enjoyed by certain individuals but a continuing 'filling up' which touches the whole congregation in an on-going way.[9] Scripture, history and contemporary experience all indicate that the Holy Spirit, not simply strategies and plans, is the one who builds the Kingdom of God. His work of renewal is threefold.

1. **He restores to its original state** a church which has drifted into a 'Do It yourself' mentality rather than seeking the guidance and empowering of God. Whilst the cultural background of the Book of Acts is very different from our own, we can learn from the dependence on the Spirit evident in the lives of the first Christians.[10]

2. **He replaces with a fresh supply** those who acknowledge their emptiness. As Christians 'give out' in service and witness so they need to receive more of God's spirit and be filled up anew.[11] The prophets spoke of the pouring out of God's Spirit which would refresh and gift God's people.[12]

3. **He arranges for a continuing validity** of our historic faith so that it is neither merely a great story from the Bible nor a personal reminiscence of something which happened to us (or a decision made) long ago. The Holy Spirit in the believer gives a vitality and holiness which should be evident to others and adds authenticity to our message.[13]

Question 1

What does Luke 5:36-38 say to your local church situation? Can you identify the 'new wine'? What new wineskins are we creating for this?

Question 2

How can we enable our church leaders to be missionary pastors?

Question 3

How can our church be a more effective missionary community?

Question 4

Where do we identify the five-fold ministry of Ephesians 4:7-8 in our congregation?

2. THE DREADED 'E' WORD - EVANGELISM?

The Bible tells the story of God's quest for the saving of a world which has disobeyed Him and gone its own way. The ten commandments, the covenant and the prophets prepare for God's rescue mission through His Son. Jesus teaches his disciples to take the message of the Kingdom to all people. Christ's crucifixion is the ultimate sign of God's determination to rescue us. Mission is therefore at the heart of the Gospel and of the character of God. His search for us and his identification with us in His Son is the model for our evangelism. Some missiologists refer to this as an incarnational approach - just as God becomes one of us in Christ, so we must identify with and be alongside others in mission[14].

Definitions of evangelism abound. Here are two helpful ones:

William Temple[15] - "To evangelise is so to present Jesus Christ in the power of the Holy Spirit, that men shall come to put their trust in him as their King in the fellowship of his church."

William Abraham[16] - "Evangelism is those actions that are governed by the intention to initiate people into the Kingdom of God".

1. Telling the Good News: Acts 10:36 - 'evaggelizesthai' - the evangel being the Gospel.
2. Bearing Witness: Acts 10:34, 41, 43 - 'marturion' - from which our word martyr is drawn.
3. Heralding the Gospel: Acts 10:42 - 'kerusso' - proclaiming and preparing the way.

Evangelism – the way in which we **declare** the Good News of Jesus.

All Christians are witnesses - evangelism is therefore not just for people with a special evangelistic gift: all have a responsibility to share the Good News. Despite astonishing church growth, mainly in the developing world, there are twice as many non-Christians in the world today as there were in 1900, so we have plenty of scope! Evangelism must therefore involve reaching out beyond the church building and must be culturally and socially relevant. Above everything it must be Holy Spirit inspired.

Mission is a broader concept. It is every way in which we **demonstrate** the Good News of Jesus: being present and active in our community for Christ's sake. Evangelism springs from this and challenges people to commitment by an open proclamation of the Gospel.

Generally speaking, our churches are usually fairly good at mission but poor at evangelism which brings people into a living relationship with God.

Question 5
How would you define evangelism and mission?

Apart from Jesus, Paul is the most outstanding evangelist in the New Testament, combining theological insight, relentless energy and pastoral care. In expounding 2 Corinthians 5, David Watson notes some of the essentials of evangelism:

v10 - Take account of the judgement of Christ.
A time of separation approaches when those who follow Christ will be saved - those who reject him will be lost. Awareness of God's judgement upon sinners was part of Paul's motivation for mission. We may feel that telling people to 'flee from the wrath to come' is old fashioned or over dramatic, but the New Testament speaks very clearly about a persons eternal destiny depending upon their commitment to Christ as Lord and Saviour.

v14 - Be motivated by the love of Christ.
Greater than the fear of judgement is the motivation that comes from the love God has first shown us in Christ, offering us free and complete forgiveness. This love enters the lives of believers and gives them a longing deep within to see others experience the love of God for themselves.

v17- Experience the power of Christ.
The power of Jesus is illustrated many times in the Gospel accounts through teaching, healing, exorcism, calming a storm, feeding 5,000 people .... Here Paul describes a spiritual transformation - a new life replacing an old life. Christ has power to change lives.

vv18-20 - Extend the ministry of Christ.
Paul speaks of a ministry of reconciliation. Just as Christ offered forgiveness and reconciliation with God, so we are to continue this ministry, which may involve sharing in his sufferings. We are representatives of the King of Kings - ambassadors -in a land where the culture is quite alien to the Kingdom of God.

v21- Focus on the death of Christ.
The cross is absolutely crucial to Paul's message. Here he describes it briefly but profoundly. Christ 'became sin for us, so that in him we might become the righteousness of God'. The cross for Paul is not just an example of noble suffering but a costly transaction which saves sinners.

Evangelism overflows from the daily life of an alive church. One of the best examples of such a mission-orientated church is that at Antioch in Acts 11:19-30 and 13:1-3:

11:26	- There the believers were first known as Christians.
11:26,30	- Converts were nurtured and equipped.
11:29	- There was an awareness of social need and a generous response to it.
13:1	- The Christian family was culturally diverse and inclusive.
13:2,3	- The church commissioned and sent out its best people in outreach.

Question 6
How can we apply this to our local church situation?

3. MOTIVES AND STYLES OF EVANGELISM

In many parts of the Book of Acts, and especially in Acts 2:37-47 and 4:32-27 we see the life of the early Christians marked by -

Koinonia — fellowship - an inclusive and diverse family;

Marturion — witness - a costly, fervent and sincere speaking out for Christ;

Diakonia — service - the love of Jesus lived out in action and meeting real needs within and beyond the Christian community;

Metanoia — change - the Holy Spirit challenged actions and attitudes; lives were radically changed.

These characteristics enable effective evangelism - evangelism was a natural overflow from the daily life of the Christian community. An emphasis on quality in the life of our church can be one factor which attracts people to Christ. Without such characteristics evangelism will have a hollow ring.

Signs of life

Bishop Michael Marshall states that "the trouble with the church today is that we no longer attempt the impossible - let alone the unexpected. We live by the cautious spirit of the age ..... We are never too disappointed, because we had never hoped for too much in the first place."[17] He lists the following characteristics as signs of life and a springboard for evangelism in the light of the coming of the Holy Spirit.

Expectation - The disciples are told to wait in expectation for the coming of the Spirit at Pentecost - Acts 1:8.

Experience - The Spirit gives a new experience of the power of God bringing joy, liberty and boldness to proclaim Christ - Acts 2:1-13.

Explanation - Peter explains that the disciples are not drunk, but that God has poured his Spirit upon them. How helpful it would be to our evangelistic task if we were called upon to explain the evidence of God's activity in people's lives! - Acts 2:14-41.

Explosion - The Spirit sent the disciples out beyond the Christian ghetto into the wider world. What will it take for us to 'break the mould' and reach people beyond 'the fringe' of the church - Acts 10:34-48.

Expansion - Any living organism must reproduce or it will become extinct. The Christian community grows as people are converted to Christ. These new converts are often the most effective evangelists as they tell their story to their friends. Acts 2:47, 4:4, 9:31 give an indication of the rapid expansion of the church.

Expression - The way the early Christians lived testified to the reality of their faith - Acts 2:42-46.

The Bible Society describes evangelism in three ways:

Presence - Being there, where people are, serving, demonstrating the use of God's Kingdom in action. Earning the right to speak out the Gospel.

Proclamation - Telling the message on the basis of being there, giving a reason for the hope that is within us as opportunity arises.

Persuasion - Bringing people to commitment on the basis of the Good News which has been proclaimed and explained.

It is crucial that we establish our motives for evangelism before formulating our methods. We need much more than just some good ideas or a wish to perpetuate the existence of our church.

Our motives for mission and evangelism may include -

Obedience to Christ's command to tell all people the message.

The final judgement of God on humankind according to His grace in Christ.

Our love for Christ and a wish that others come to know him too.

A desire to see society changed for the better, according to God's righteous standards.

We have Good News to share and we cannot keep it to ourselves for it thrills us so much.

Question 7
What motivates you for mission and what hampers you?

4. FAITH SHARING

Faith sharing is rooted in an incarnational approach to mission - 'Being there' amongst people, not retreating into a Christian ghetto. Jesus lived his life mainly among ordinary people and occasionally went aside to be with the faithful. Often our models for sharing our faith seem the opposite of this - occasional forays out of the safety of the church: a kind of 'hit and run' approach. Jesus, Emmanuel (God with us) missioned by sharing the everyday experiences of ordinary people and through this involvement, demonstrating the in-breaking of God's Kingdom.

How can we then follow Jesus' model of mission through that involvement, demonstrating the in-breaking of God's Kingdom? Here are some credentials for sharing your faith.

Sure - knowing what you believe - especially important in a multi-faith society.

Simple - clear in presentation. Think through how you can clearly express your faith and practise telling your story to a Christian friend.

Sympathetic - care about the person you are speaking to and try to understand 'where they are coming from' without in any way patronizing them.

Systematic - covering the key elements of the Gospel. Be focused on the cross and resurrection. Explain the terms you use, avoiding religious jargon.

Surrendered - inspired by prayer. Only God can change hearts and lives. We must submit to His power and His will and pray for those to whom we witness.

Becoming a disciple is usually a process with various stages rather than a single dramatic event or sudden crisis. Even some of the great examples of 'sudden'conversion, such as Paul, have several stages leading them to faith.

Here is a process that many came through on their faith journey. You could apply this to many Biblical characters (e.g. Zacchaeus in Luke 19:1-10) but also to your own experience:

Complacency - "I can't be bothered to consider this."
Curiosity - "I'll look into this."
Conviction - "I really should act on this."
Commitment - "I'll do it now."
Change - "I'll put things right with God's help."

The journey of faith is not as neat and tidy as this may suggest. However, if through our witness we are able to move people along this scale we will be achieving significant things for the Kingdom of God.

To take another example, consider Simon Peter. At what stage does he become Christian? When he is 'called' by Jesus and leaves his nets, or on the Mount of Transfiguration or in the courtyard as the cock crows, or at the empty tomb, or at Pentecost, or after his vision of the Gospel for the Gentiles in Acts 10? Discipleship and conversion for Peter is a process, with several crucial steps along the way.

Question 8
To what extent is your story ('testimony,) a process? Identify some of the most significant events on your faith journey.

A more detailed description indicating a similar process towards commitment and moving on from there as a disciple of Christ is the Engel Scale[18].

- 10	|	Awareness of the supernatural
- 9	|	No effective knowledge of Christianity
- 8	|	Initial awareness of Christianity
- 7	|	Interest in Christianity
- 6	|	Awareness of the basic facts of the Gospel
- 5	|	Grasp of the implications of the Gospel
- 4	|	Positive attitude to the Gospel
- 3	|	Awareness of personal need
- 2	|	Challenge and decision to act
- 1	|	Repentance and faith
	|	**A NEW DISCIPLE IS BORN**
+ 1	|	Evaluation of decision
+ 2	|	Initiation into the church
+ 3	|	Helping introduce others to Christ
.	|	Growth of understanding of faith
.	|	Growth of Christian character
.	|	Discovery and use of gifts
.	|	Christian life style

·		Stewardship of resources
·		Prayer
·		Openness to others
·		Effective sharing of faith

We may feel uncomfortable with such a precise breakdown of stages but nevertheless the point is made that most people become Christians through a gradual process rather than a sudden crisis. Engel also stresses the importance of spiritual growth and nurture after conversion.

Sharing your faith

Some people are at a loss to know where to begin witnessing. Either they can't think of many receptive people or the size of the task just seems too daunting.

Here are some of the spheres in which you live and where you can witness to your faith:

- home
- work
- social life
- school - college
- neighbours
- church
- neighbourhood groups

Question 9

Can you identify people in these spheres, pray for them and witness to them as God provides the opportunities? You might want to write a prayer diary, putting one or two names against these various headings and remembering them regularly in your prayers, asking that God will give you the opportunity to speak to them of Him and that you will say and do the right thing at the right time.

There are some remarkably relevant examples of faith sharing in the New Testament, showing how faith is communicated naturally from the point at which the hearer has already reached in their understanding and life experience. Jesus' meeting with the woman at the well in John 4 and Philip's witness to the Ethiopian on the desert road in Acts 8:26-40 are classic examples of faith sharing[19].

Question 10

What do these two examples tell us about effective faith sharing?

17

4. A STRATEGY FOR EVANGELISM IN THE LOCAL CHURCH

Evangelism cannot be defined only in terms of one person sharing their faith with another. Though this is a key area, it is important for the local church to be geared to winning people for Christ. Often churches have lost sight of this goal and are more concerned with maintaining their present activities than reaching out into their neighbourhood. Moving from a maintenance to a mission mode begins with taking an audit of our present situation, which will provide the basic facts for appropriate goal setting. We need objective information about:

1. **Our community** - areas of change, growth, need and opportunity.
2. **Our church** - our key activities, the things we do well, the things we must improve on.
3. **Our gospel** – What we believe about the Gospel. Put in a sentence the message we wish to get across[20].

Question 11
Ask "Why is this church here?". Having done this you can formulate your mission statement - It might begin: "this church exists to ....".

A church in which I ministered defined its mission in these terms:
"This church exists to be the people of God,
    worshipping him,
    sharing the Good News,
    serving others".
Having done that the congregation and leadership had to define more precisely their goals under these headings and monitor progress regularly.

Writing in the 'Church Growth Digest'[21], David Pitts suggests that a good mission statement should:
  i. **Be portable.** People should be able to carry it in their memories.
 ii. **Have direction.** It should carry within it a suggestion as to what further action should be taken to implement it.
iii. **Define what the organisation does.** Be clear as to what basic business the organisation is in.
 iv. **Make clear who the organisation exists for.** The church is said to be "the only organisation which exists for the benefit of its non-members". Is this really the case?

v. **Articulate the manner in which the mission is to be conducted.** The core values of the organisation should be reflected in its mission statement. Declining organisations have a tendency to amalgamate and restructure when in fact they need to return to their founding dream.

Once you have established the facts and identified the task, you can move on to set the goals.

A church's goals should aim directly to implement its mission statement. They are practical ways of achieving its stated purposes. Goals should be both short term (6 - 12 months) and longer term (up to 5 years). Make your goals as specific as you can.

Roy Pointer offers the following guidance on setting goals[22]. Goals should be:

i.   **Relevant** - related to accomplishing the task.

ii.   **Measurable** - allowing us to know how and when we have accomplished the goal.

iii. **Achievable** - be within our resources to achieve.

iv.   **Significant** - make a difference to our situation.

v.   **Personal** - involve those who set the goals in meeting them.

The next step is to equip the members.

Your mission statement and goals will have been formulated with your members' gifts and experience in mind, but if those members are to own and apply them there must be good communication. One of the main reasons for visionary leadership not effecting radical change is an inability in communicating ideas appropriately beyond the boundaries of the innovators and risk takers to the potential adopters in the middle ground.

It is vital that the vision is constantly, clearly and imaginatively communicated to everyone in the church. Have the mission statement on posters and notice sheets. Refer often to the goals currently being pursued. Be clear and practical about ways in which people can contribute towards their achievement. Alongside this plan, arrange relevant training of church members which affirms people's gifts rather than giving a guilt trip based on past failures in missionary endeavour.

Greater knowledge and ability bring greater confidence and commitment. Specific goals are unlikely to be achieved without specific training in those skills and activities needed to achieve them, but building people's confidence is crucial. This can be achieved through pastoral support but also through enabling people to have hands on involvement in specific aspects of evangelism.

Keep reviewing progress - make adjustments accordingly and ask how far and effectively goals have been achieved.

PAUL'S METHODS IN MISSION
Paul didn't have a formalised mission policy but his strategy is clear from reading the record of his missionary work in the Book of Acts and in his own letters.

1. **Adapted strategy to locality** - 1 Cor 9:16-23.
   The Gospel must be interpreted for the hearers in ways they understand and relate to.

2. **Went to all strata of society** - Rom 1:14, 15.
   Some sections of our society are virtually unevangelised – young people, ethnic minorities, the 'working classes'.

3. **Championed the cause of the Gentiles** - Gal 3:28.
   He was prepared to go to those who were looked down upon and ignored by the religious people of his day.

4. **Concentrated on strategic cities** - Rom 1:10.
   Rome, Ephesus, Corinth and Thessalonica were commercial and cultural crossroads. Evangelism carried out there could have a wide impact, not just among their citizens but through them in the places to which they travelled.

5. **Used the local church as a base** - 1 Thess 1:7,8.
   Establishing one church became a springboard for mission into a wide area around it where new congregations were later planted. He also remained answerable to those who commissioned him.

6. **Proclaimed a full Gospel** - Acts 20:27.
   Teaching in depth consolidated the faith of recent converts. Jesus was not white, middle class, Methodist or culturally bound. Sadly our evangelism seems to have ignored this and has instead domesticated and diminished the Gospel.

7. **Had complete confidence in the message** - Rom 1:15.
   He knew what he believed and was able to put it over effectively to his hearers. Conviction communicated.

8. **Nurtured believers towards maturity** - Col 1:28; 2:6-7
   Paul looked for disciples, not just converts. His letters were written to help Christians grow in their faith.

9. **Consolidated earlier work** - Acts 15:30,36.
   Return visits were deliberately planned to build up recently established churches and ensure sound teaching.

10. **Set an example to be followed** - 1 Cor 11:1.
    Paul himself modelled the mission he was engaged in and the Lord he

served. Many people may disagree with us but they should not doubt our integrity.

11. **Trained young leaders** - 1 Tim 4:8.
Much of Paul's letter writing was concerned with preparing to hand over the task to properly trained younger people who would continue the work after him. Mentoring and apprenticeship was a deliberate strategy.

12. **Maintained a pioneering spirit** - 2 Cor 10:15-17.
His enthusiasm and vision is infectious and no doubt challenged many younger workers. He has hopes and plans even when surrounded by constraints and personal limitations.

Question 12
Which aspects of Paul's mission strategy are most relevant to us today?

6. MODELS FOR MISSION

If mission is to be more than spasmodic efforts by individuals and small groups of enthusiasts, we must have a church life which allows for growth and change. Here are three models which illustrate different approaches.

The 'Come' Model

This is the approach to mission which may be well meaning but is actually very out of touch with the way society responds to religion today. The members say, "We're here and you're very welcome to joins us" - They even put "All welcome" on all their posters!

A few new people trickle into this church from time to time but overall the faithful are left asking the question: "Why don't they come like they used to?" and stories are told of how the place used to be bursting at the seams for the Sunday School Anniversary. What has not been appreciated is that the world has moved on and the church has not, leading to an ever increasing and unbridged gap between the two. Though there are a few exceptions, it is largely ineffective to do evangelism entirely through a welcome poster on a noticeboard or a leaflet dropped through a letterbox describing the activities of the wonderfully friendly church around the corner. Incidentally, almost every church considers itself friendly. The best people to ask about that are the people who don't go!

The 'Come' model then has an unrealistic view of a secular materialistic society. It assumes that people will come to the activities offered at church (either Sunday or on weekdays) if we advertise them well: choir, housegroup, social events, children's and youth clubs, Sunday School, worship ..... This model is inward looking, complacent and focused on church programmes (and problems). Consequently it makes little impact on the neighbourhood and attracts only 'religious' people. Many new congregations have been planted on this Christendom model with little appreciation of the huge gap between society and church. We must be careful not to reproduce models of being church which have already failed to connect with the communities they are called to reach.

"We're here and you are welcome to join us."

Fellowship Groups   Worship

Choir   Socials

Junior Church   Meetings & Committees

Children's/Youth Activities

The 'Go' Model

Aware of the failure of the 'Come' model, some swing to the opposite extreme with a flurry of activity which takes the church into the community. "We're coming to meet you where you are." The non-church person, feeling threatened by this approach, keeps their distance -"Look out, the Bible thumpers are coming" is their reaction. Genuine Christian zeal is interpreted by the observers as "We're coming to get you". Talk of crusade and campaign sounds alien, confrontational and paternalistic.

Nevertheless this 'Go' model does make an impact and faith is evidenced in some unlikely places. Discussion groups and quizzes are held in pub and club lounges, worship is taken into the local community hall and a new congregation is in embryo there. Door to door visitation and gospel distribution takes place, and a drop-in for lonely people is started, as well as a youth club run by church members grounded on detached youth outreach. A team from the 'Go' church leads school assemblies and starts a children's club with the contacts made. Then there are 'open airs' in the park and the shopping centre and a march of witness. It really is 'all happening'! The problem is that although people are becoming Christians, some of the key workers are at the point of collapse. There seems to be an emphasis on the amount and not the quality of activity: burn out syndrome has set in and fragmentation of effort results. This model tends to be programme rather than relationally orientated, despite the widely acknowledged fact that around 85% of Christians come to faith through the witness of a friend or a member of their family.[23]

We need to balance outreach with personal and corporate spiritual growth. Whilst we grow through the experience of mission, through sharing our faith and involvement in various projects, we need to be refreshed and strengthened for the task by strong fellowship and teaching at base and by 'time off' with our families - our primary mission field and one too often neglected.

The 'Go' model captures the vision and pioneer spirit of the enthusiasts and puts mission at the top of the church's agenda, but this may be at the expense of worship and personal development, especially if the minister is the energy behind it. Some outreach activities may be isolated from the life of the parent church and therefore lose the prayer and practical support of all but a small section of the congregation. A church leadership obsessed with outreach may neglect the pastoral support of the existing congregation. In the local church we need the pastor-evangelists, not just among the ordained ministry but throughout the congregation, which recaptures the apostolic model of a church existing for the benefit of its non-members.

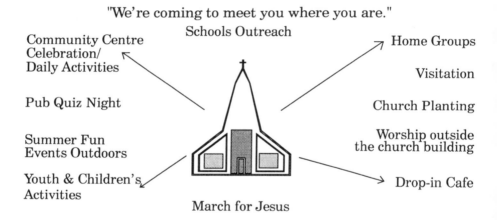

"We're coming to meet you where you are."

Schools Outreach

Community Centre
Celebration/
Daily Activities

Pub Quiz Night

Summer Fun
Events Outdoors

Youth & Children's
Activities

Home Groups

Visitation

Church Planting

Worship outside
the church building

Drop-in Cafe

March for Jesus

The 'Enabling' Model

We have described two extreme and opposite models of being church. Clearly we need to combine the better aspects of both in a way which enables outreach whilst strengthening the existing congregation. The enabling model may seem idealistic - but is there anything wrong with having ideals? It attempts to witness to society from within that society: being 'in the flow' of daily living rather than shouting louder from its isolated pond.

Here we have a congregation whose inspirational worship (no particular style is envisaged), relevant meetings and committees, effective youth and children's ministry and biblically based teaching and training resources its outreach. Much mission planning tries to 'hit' the neighbourhood before seeking the renewal of the church. A church can never be fully 'ready' for a period of mission - we will wait forever for that. Nevertheless, in order to be motivated for outreach and ready to receive new believers and disciple them, a church must have the right spiritual facilities. We do not put new born babies in a fridge! When planning a mission, it may be necessary to have a mission to the church (an 'in-reach') before a mission to the community (an 'outreach').

The enabling model aims to increase prayer power, deepen biblical understanding and keep the church roof on in order to mission. The activities inside facilitate those outside. Outreach draws people into the church and equips them to return to the world with the Gospel. There is a mutual support and encouragement within the whole Christian family for evangelist and pastoral worker alike.

This model requires good communication, sensible delegation and mature management skills. It requires a team approach to ministry and an identification and use of spiritual gifts. It is this kind of local church which will have an effect for the Kingdom far greater than special projects and campaigns (which have their place) for it will have a long term vision and it will engage the gifts of a larger proportion of the congregation. It will have a wholistic view of mission with varied styles of being church for varied cultural locations and groups. It will release its members from an endless round of 'churchy' meetings to be 'church dispersed in community', affirming and supporting Christians in their workplace and homes, giving them time to build friendships which earn the right to share the faith. The enabling church is distinctive from society, yet engaged with it.[24]

"Our vibrant fellowship fires and resources our mission."

Schools Outreach

Youth Outreach

Community Celebrations

Inspirational Worship

Visitation

Effective Youth/ Children's Work

Church Planting

Supportive Fellowship

Relevant Meetings & Committees

Biblical Teaching & Training

Drop-in

Outdoor Events

Home Groups

Question 13: *Which of these models describes your church? How can Christians be 'distinctive from but engaged with' society?*

Question 14: *How can our church programme reflect the needs for personal spiritual growth and also for outreach? Do we expect people to meet us on our turf and on our terms?*

7. MOBILISING THE LOCAL CHURCH FOR MISSION -

George Carey states several characteristics of a growing church[25]:

- It is prepared to face disturbing news – grasping some nettles concerning the challenges we face and the things that are not working.
- It is more concerned with God's Mission than with its own existence – we are not here to sustain an institution but to declare God's Kingdom.
- It is geared to the deepening of faith – many churches need to strengthen their discipleship training and nurture of believers.
- It harnesses the ministry of all its members – working as a team.
- It aims for quality in worship – not one particular style but an investment of time and creative energy into offering meaningful and inspiring worship.

Towards a Growing Church

The Bible Society has conducted extensive research on church growth over the past 25 years and suggest the following points which enable growth[26]:

Constant Prayer - This has been the root of all historic revivals but is often lacking in local churches. Individual members may be faithful prayer warriors, but corporate prayer is restricted to Sunday services. It is difficult to get a large church prayer meeting off the ground, but it should be possible to establish a network of small prayer groups in homes. These may be given a specific focus each week, through a prayer and notice sheet distributed to the whole congregation.

Respect for Biblical authority - Virtually all growing churches across the denominations are those where the authority and reliability of the Bible is upheld and there is an openness to the Holy Spirit.

Effective leadership – Strong, purposeful leadership with an emphasis on disciple training, team work and delegation of responsibilities will enable growth. It is possible to combine pastoral care and evangelism, in fact pastoral contacts often provide an excellent mission field.

Mobilised membership - A team approach enables each member to discover and use their gifts. Burdens are shared and Christians grow in faith and experience.

Eventful worship - Predictability rather than surprise mark much of what we do in church but an encounter with God will affirm the reality of worship, whatever particular style that worship takes.

Continuous evangelism - Churches need to focus on **being** a mission rather than **having** a mission. Evangelism should be a central and natural part of the church's function. All churches are witnesses. It is not a question of whether to witness but **how** to witness.

Community life - The message proclaimed will be demonstrated in everyday life - in a concern for truth, peace and justice; in neighbourhood involvement and in the fellowship of believers itself.

Compassionate service - Action inspired by love going alongside verbal proclamation. By being alongside people and caring about them we earn the right to speak of what Christ means to us.

Openness to change - New Christians will change the comfortable, traditional nature of the local church by their vitality and their questions. There must be a willingness to be flexible, whilst retaining what is best in established ways.

Released resources - The Holy Spirit gifts every Christian, but these gifts are often suppressed and need to be released so that the whole body of Christ functions as it should. We need a willingness to receive and use these gifts.

Churches decline for several reasons:
These are highlighted by the Church Growth Movement as:

Nominality - People who may have some church connection but have no live personal commitment. Some may have drifted away from a faith they once professed, others will have never believed or attended church but would be horrified to be thought of as 'non-Christian', whilst having very little idea of what a Christian actually is.

Private religion - Some churchgoers hide behind a 'smoke screen' of privacy. They feel embarrassed to express their faith to others, probably because of fear of what others may think of them, but mainly because they realise that they have little to say, for they have little personal experience of God.

Lack of involvement - An unwillingness to be part of activities which involve spiritual encounter is common. Some church activities actually enable people to hide from God rather than encountering Him. Church leaders may be unwilling to delegate work which could be done by others, resulting in churches which seem like a flight in a plane - a lot of people sitting back and looking bored and a small number of others rushing about doing everything.

Irrelevant church programme - Activities arranged entertain those used to church life but are completely alien to the majority. The 'Come' model has no impact on society at large.

Church programme too full - Committees, Bible studies and other church events take up so much time in many situations that members have little free time to build and maintain the necessary bridges with neighbours, friends and even family, so opportunities for witness disappear.

Low self-esteem - A failure syndrome may suggest that we are not ready or not good enough to evangelise but instead of putting things right, inertia sets in. Pastoral support and careful discipling can help people recover confidence in the Gospel and in the knowledge that God can and will use their gifts. Confidence is crucial.

What can the church leader(s) do?

Whilst mission must be owned by the whole congregation, a great deal can be achieved by strong, sensitive leadership. We especially need pastor-evangelists who:

1. Have a passion for evangelism - a zeal to reach those right outside the orbit of the church.

2. Teach it - through biblical preaching, seminars or house groups, applied to the modern secular world.

3. Model it - inspiration will be 'caught' by other people as they see the leader's personal witness and communication skills in a variety of settings and learn from them.

4. Encourage prayer, friendship, love and concern for the neighbourhood within the congregation. A live and caring Christian family will attract others.

5. Develop real worship. No particular style is needed. What is vital is that people encounter God.

6. Build a committed core. A leadership team made up of people with a vision for the church, who are themselves growing in faith, will minister more effectively than one person ever can. Others can be drawn in by the members of the team.

7. Appoint those whom God chooses and equips. These may not be the 'obvious' choices, nor are they merely volunteers. Those who God calls He enables to do the work He has for them.

8. Teach openness to the Holy Spirit. Leaders who listen to what God is saying to them today, rather than relying on what they did in the past, will have the prophetic role which is needed.

9. Involve all kinds of people and use their gifts. Avoid a monochrome membership. Diversity brings its tensions but this should be a strength rather than a weakness.

10. Offer training in personal evangelism. A short practical course can be an enormous help and encouragement to diffident disciples who are not too sure where to begin.

What any Christian can do:

1. Maintain your own spiritual life. A strong daily devotional life of prayer and Bible reading gives the resources needed for active witness.

2. Be an encourager. Positive attitudes and a word to build up and help those who lead, especially new leaders.

3. Be willing to serve. Willingness to do seemingly menial tasks follows Jesus' example of humbly washing the disciples' feet.

4. Make friends outside the church and have an attractive life style - too many Christians are just plain boring!.

5. Be willing to speak of Christ and practice telling your story with a Christian friend, so that when you have opportunity you will be clear in your presentation.

6. Use and test your gifts but also try to draw others in to work with you.

What can the whole church do?

1. Quality worship. High expectations and prayerful preparation for worship by the congregation will improve the experience of worship.

2. Love displayed in the whole Christian family conveys a warmth which makes people feel accepted.

3. Strategy for mission needs to be worked out practically by setting targets and later renewing progress.

4. Enable all God's people to discover and use their gifts and so grow into mature Christians.[27]

Question 15
How can our church be more effective in mission?

A live church in action - Acts 3-8

The early Christian community grew rapidly as the survey of Acts 3-8 below indicates, though it was not without problems. Here are some of its key characteristics[28].

Signs and wonders	:	3:1-10
Repent and receive	:	3:11-26
Opposition and apologetic	:	4:1-22
Believing prayer	:	4:23-31
Unity and caring	:	4:32-37
Discipline and judgement	:	5:1-11
Supernatural healing	:	5:12-16
Costly witness	:	5:17-41
Shared leadership	:	6:1-7
Light and darkness	:	6:8-15
Biblical preaching	:	7:1-53
Ultimate sacrifice	:	7:54 - 8:1

Question 16
Which elements of this Biblical model of mission are most pertinent to us?

What can we do?

Here are some things which have proved effective in various situations. They are in no particular order of importance except that those early in the list relate to the church itself and those appearing later are increasingly geared to those at present outside.

- Improve pastoral visiting programme of existing church contacts
- Biblical teaching and preaching
- Re-vitalise children - youth - uniformed groups
- Good worship
- Renewed leadership
- Network of prayer groups
- Church and community audit
- New house group programme

- Church weekend away or caring-sharing weekend
- Lunch club
- Visiting the elderly
- Celebration event
- Worship in homes
- Men's breakfast
- Training in personal evangelism
- Youth camp
- All age worship group
- Door to door visiting
- Close your church building and open a shop front mission
- Street theatre
- After school club
- Lead school assemblies
- Quiz night in a pub
- March for Jesus
- Exhibition in a public building
- Carols in the Shopping Centre
- Family centre work
- Youth group meeting in a chip shop
- Plant a new congregation

Under the Holy Spirit's inspiration you will need programmes which both **build up** the existing congregation and **reach out** to the community at large.[29]

Question 17
Are there things here that we might prayerfully consider attempting as part of our mission strategy in the next twelve months?

8. BUILDING A CHURCH FOR THE UNCHURCHED

In the West today most people are IGnostics not AGnostics – ignorant concerning Christianity rather than undecided about it; they really don't have the information to make an informed decision about Christ. Most church debates are irrelevant - they address questions which are not fundamental - ordination of women, creation or evolution, sacramental theology, etc. The church and church leaders have a poor public image (soap opera vicars) - consequently people reject the packaging, without considering the product. Most Christian speakers make huge assumptions about where people are at in terms of Biblical background, ethics etc: "Last week we looked at eschatology in Thessalonians, today it's incarnation from Isaiah" isn't designed to grab the attention of many people!

We must scratch where people itch. Postmodernity is more interested in life before death than life after death - i.e. what being a Christian can mean now. Does it work, rather than is it true? There is greater awareness of doubt than guilt. We need to answer questions like "Why am I here?" more often than "How can my sins be forgiven?". We may need to bring someone to Christ before we bring them to church; Sunday morning service is probably not the best time and place for evangelism, yet sometimes it seems to be the only one. Christians need to meet people on their ground - pubs, homes, sports clubs. If Jesus were on earth today, it is likely that he would spend more time in pubs than in churches because that is where the 'ordinary' people are to be found. He was called a 'winebibber' and a 'friend of sinners'. We have to win people's confidence since many people are distrustful of Christians who they may equate with tele-evangelists or wimps.

Empty success as much as unemployment drags down self-esteem where worth is interpreted in terms of what you do for a living. Some therefore feel that life is pointless or that the world is out of control. Christians have a great opportunity here. We must affirm that God is in control and that He has a purpose for our lives but we will need to interpret what we mean by terms such as 'King' and 'Lord'. Unpacking Christian jargon may help us understand faith in order to interpret it for others.

The American missiologist, George Hunter III, in his book *How to Reach Secular People*[30] asks, "Who are those to reach secular people?" They are those who:
1. understand the movements of modern culture;
2. live by the faith they commend;
3. have a passion for a missionary church;
4. do not write people off as being uninterested or unable to turn to Christ
5. identify with the people they are called to reach;

6. encourage the church to witness in word and deed, showing the signs of the kingdom;
7. engage in Christian apologetics, giving reasoned answers to genuine questions and doubts posed by non-Christians.

If we are to reach the unchurched we must -
1. Seek opportunities to give people an understanding of Christian basics. People must have information on which later to make a decision.
2. Encourage discussion not lectures - answer real questions, not supposed ones. Conducting a questionnaire survey of religious beliefs will help you know 'where people are coming from'.
3. Invite people to accept a challenge - don't water it down apologetically.
4. Don't hide unpalatable truths - encourage dialogue on these.
5. Develop friendships with non-Christians, provide support groups for evangelists and nurture for new Christians. Use social networks as a means of reaching people.
6. Be culturally appropriate, use plain English - any fool can use long words.
7. Plant churches - it is estimated that 20,000 new churches are needed to evangelise Britain.

Question 18
How can we best reach those right outside the church?

Church planting
Church Planting was a strategy of the early church, of nineteenth century Methodism and of the overseas missionary movement. Church Growth thinking encourages the 'multiplication of congregations' as a means of evangelism. Methodism in Britain currently begins a new congregation every month but closes a church building every four days.

In this context, some church leaders dismiss the church planting movement on the basis that there are 45,000 congregations in Britain already, many in buildings which certainly have space for more to attend. This is of course perfectly true but most churches are 'come' structures, expecting people to come to them. The church plant aims to take the kingdom out into the community. Many places in Britain are 'unchurched' with no church building or alive church in the vicinity. Some of these are new housing areas, others may be places from which the church has withdrawn, (e.g. Asian areas of British cities perceived as 'no go' areas for evangelism) or where it has never had a strong presence (e.g. council housing estates).

Stuart Christine states:

"Church planting is precisely about the establishing of a living relevant witness within every people group, so that all may be offered a realistic opportunity (to hear the Gospel).... It is the job of churches to plant churches .... as the outworking of strategy."[31]

Church planting has been most common among newer denominations - Pentecostal, house churches, independent churches. On the other hand, 53% of Anglican churches were established before 1500 and most Methodist churches have their origins in the nineteenth century, and assume their congregation is the primary model of being church. Recent church planting, however, suggests that smaller cells which commit themselves to growth and dividing to form new cells after perhaps eighteen months are more effective in reaching unchurched people.

A great variety of models of church planting are possible. The following are two examples:

(1) The creation of one or more 'daughter' churches, retaining a link with the 'mother' congregation - a traditional Anglican pattern

(2) Multiple congregations within one building - offering varied and distinctive styles to suit different needs, cultures and preferences.

Effective church planting springs out of strength, vision and careful planning,.

Favourable factors for church planting from within the local church include:
- Increased spiritual confidence
- Increased community consciousness
- Increased inter-church co-operation
- Renewal and growth in the congregation
- Vision of individuals conveyed to a planting group and to the whole church.

A geographically central or accessible location is needed, distant from other churches. Leaders need to be released from the sending church. Planting may take place across cultural boundaries. These are as real for college trained leaders on a council estate as for the white missionary in an African village. This can lead to a problem in enabling local people to take on responsibility if the planting team pull out. Planting to the same culture is usually more successful. A team approach to leadership is important. There are strong New Testament precedents for this, but not all pioneering visionaries are comfortable in a team.[32]

It is better to speak of new congregations than new churches since church may convey 'building' and the plant may use an existing church or community building. Also the emphasis is on people not bricks. Whatever building you use, make sure it's user friendly - warm, light, decent seating, cheerful and accessible .....[33]

Church planting is not just pragmatism, it is theology in action: mission alongside people modelled on the ministry of Jesus[34]. **In all our strategies and ideas it is important to understand that what most churches need is not a new strategy or a new idea but new life through God's Holy Spirit.** We should not be looking for a revival of past glories but a fresh renewing and a resurrection of hope and life.

Question 19
Is the establishment of a new congregation appropriate in any way in our situation?

Question 20
If so, what form might this take?

NOTES

1. 1 Peter 3:15

2. William Abraham, *The Logic of Evangelism*, Hodder & Stoughton 1989

3 Matthew 28:19-20

4. Eddie Gibbs, *The God Who Communicates*, Hodder 1985

5. Lyle Schaller & Kennon Callaghan, *Effective Church Leadership*, Abingdon 1989

6. George Barna, *User Friendly Churches*, Regal Books, Ventura 1991

7. Luke 5:36-38.

8. Michael Green, *Evangelism through the Local Church*, Hodder 1990

9. Ephesians 4:1-6

10. Acts 2:1-13

11. Ephesians 3:19 & 5:18

12. Joel 2:28

13. Galatians 5:22-23

14. Isaiah 7:14 - Immanuel, 'God with us'

15. William Temple - *Towards the Conversion of England*, Church Assembly Board 1945

16. William Abraham, *The Art of Evangelism*, Cliff College Publishing, 1993

17. Michael Marshall, *Expectations for Evangelism*, Bible Reading Fellowship 1991

18. J F Engel, *What's gone wrong with the harvest?*, Zondervan 1982

19. Philip A Clarke, *Being A Mission Church*, Cliff College Publishing 1994

20. Brian Hoare, *Developing a Strategy for Evangelism in the Local Church*, Connect 1994

21. Church Growth Digest, Vol.14, No.2
22. Roy Pointer, *How Do Churches Grow?*, Marc Europe 1984

23. John Finney, *Finding Faith Today*, Bible Society 1992

24. Robert Warren, *Being Human, Being Church*, Triangle 1995

25. George Carey, *I Believe*, SPCK 1991

26. Roy Pointer, *How Do Churches Grow?*, Marshalls 1984
    Eddie Gibbs, *Winning Them Back*, Monarch 1993

27. J Drane, *Evangelism for a New Age*, Marshall Pickering 1994

28. F F Bruce, *The Book of Acts*, New London Commentaries, MMS 1954
    I H Marshall, *Acts*, IVP 1980
    J R W Stott, *The Message of Acts*, IVP 1990

29. G Howard Mellor, *The Good News Works*, Home Mission 1991
    Philip A Clarke, *Preparing for Mission*, Cliff College Publishing 1995

30. George Hunter III, *How To Reach Secular People*, Abingdon 1991

31. M Robinson & S Christine, *Planting Tomorrow's Churches Today* Monarch 1992

32. R Hopkins, *Church Planting*, Grove Booklets on Evangelism 4, 1992

33. G Horsley, *Planting New Congregations*, Methodist Church Home Mission Division 1994.
    Stopping the Rot Video, Methodist Church 1996

34. P Nodding, *Local Church Planting*, Marshall 1994
    S Murray, Church Planting, Oxford 1998

BIBLIOGRAPHY:

Among the many recent books on mission and evangelism the following are recommended:

W Abraham,	*The Art of Evangelism,*	Cliff College Publishing 1993
P Brierley,	*Reaching and Keeping Teenagers,*	Marc 1993
P Clarke,	*Jesus at Tesco,*	Cliff College Publishing 1997
J Drane,	*Evangelism for a New Age,*	Marshall Pickering 1994
J Finney,	*Finding Faith Today,*	Bible Society 1992
E Fox & G Morris,	*Faith Sharing,*	Discipleship Resources, 1996
E Gibbs,	*I Believe in Church Growth,*	Hodder 1981
D Hilbourne,	*Picking up the Pieces,*	IVP 1996
G Hunter III,	*How to Reach Secular People,*	Abingdon 1992
S Murray,	*Church Planting,*	Paternoster 1998
L Newbigin,	*Foolishness to the Greeks,*	Eerdmans 1986
N Pollard,	*Evangelism Made Slightly Less Difficult,*	IVP 1997
P Richter & L Francis,	*Gone but not Forgotten,*	DLT 1998
M Riddell,	*Threshold of the Future,*	SPCK 1997
M Robinson,	*To Win the West,*	Monarch 1996
J Sanders,	*No Other Name,*	Eerdmans 1992
A Walker,	*Telling the Story,*	SPCK 1996
R Warren,	*Being Human, Being Church,*	Marshall 1995
D Watson,	*I Believe in Evangelism,*	Hodder & Stoughton 1976
D Wells,	*God in the Wasteland,*	IVP 1994